# RAISING THE FLAG

## HOW A PHOTOGRAPH GAVE A NATION HOPE IN WARTIME

by Michael Burgan

Content Adviser: Edward Segel, PhD, Professor,
Department of History, Reed College

Reading Adviser: Alexa L. Sandmann, EdD, Professor of
Literacy, College and Graduate School of Education, Health,
and Human Services, Kent State University

COMPASS POINT BOOKS
a capstone imprint

Compass Point Books
151 Good Counsel Drive
P.O. Box 669
Mankato, MN 56002-0669

Editor: Jennifer Fretland VanVoorst
Designer: Tracy Davies
Media Researcher: Wanda Winch
Library Consultant: Kathleen Baxter
Production Specialist: Sarah Bennett

## Image Credits

AP Images, 25, Joe Rosenthal, 52, John Rous, 47, 57 (bottom), U.S. Marine Corps,
32; Corbis: Ed Kashi, 39; DoD photo by U.S. Navy/Phan Lee McCaskill, 21, 57 (top);
Getty Images Inc: Time Life Pictures/W. Eugene Smith, 34, Time Life Pictures/US
Marine Corps/Louis R. Lowery, 36, U.S. Coast Guard, 6; Library of Congress, Prints
and Photographs Division, 10, 12, 15; Marine Corps Historical Center, 40-41, 59;
NARA: Joe Rosenthal, cover, 9, 31, 55, Marine Corps/Dreyfuss, 7, Navy, 13, 17, 56,
U.S. Coast Guard, 22, U.S. Marine Corps, 42; Naval Historic Foundation, 5, 27, D.G.
Christian, 18, USMC/Staff Sergeant Louis R. Lowery, 37, USMCR/Warrant Officer
Obie Newcomb Jr., 24; Newscom: Republic Pictures, 50, 58 (left); Shutterstock:
Kenneth Graff, 45, Michael G. Smith, 48, 58 (right); Wikipedia: Jeff Dahl, 30, Mark
Pellegrinni, 29.

 This book was manufactured with paper containing
at least 10 percent post-consumer waste.

## Library of Congress Cataloging-in-Publication Data

Burgan, Michael.
  Raising the flag : how a photograph gave a nation hope in wartime / by Michael
Burgan.
       p. cm. — (Compass point books. Captured history)
  Summary: "Explores and analyzes the historical context and significance of the
iconic Joe Rosenthal photograph"—Provided by publisher.
  Includes bibliographical references and index.
  ISBN 978-0-7565-4395-2 (library binding)
  ISBN 978-0-7565-4449-2 (paperback)
  1. Iwo Jima, Battle of, Japan, 1945—Juvenile literature. 2. World War, 1939–
1945—Photography—Juvenile literature. 3. Rosenthal, Joe, 1911–2006—Juvenile
literature. I. Title. II. Series.
  D767.99.I9B867 2011
  940.54'2528—dc22                                    2010038572

Visit Compass Point Books on the Internet at *www.capstonepub.com*

Printed in the United States of America in North Mankato, Minnesota.
092010      005933CGS11

# TABLE OF CONTENTS

## Chapter One

# BATTLE FOR IWO JIMA

On the morning of February 19, 1945, the big guns of U.S. Navy warships near the island of Iwo Jima began to boom. They fired huge shells filled with explosives. Smaller guns also bombarded the target. The bursting of the shells and the swirling dust they stirred darkened the sky.

The guns were just the first part of the American assault on the Japanese island, which is in the western Pacific Ocean. Around 8 a.m. the guns fell silent as the roar of warplanes filled the air. Some dropped bombs while others fired rockets and machine guns as they flew over the island. When the planes had finished their mission, the big guns at sea opened fire again.

Amid the noise, smoke, and commotion, two groups of men waited for battle. On hundreds of ships, 110,000 U.S. Marines prepared to go ashore. The first wave of them was on the small boats that would take them to the beach. Then the Marines would do what they had trained to do and had already done so well during World War II. Their mission was to take Iwo Jima from the other group of waiting men—the roughly 21,000 Japanese soldiers dug into the island.

The Japanese faced difficult odds. The Marines were well supplied and greatly outnumbered them. But the Japanese knew every part of Iwo Jima. And they had prepared for this invasion for months. Their commander, Tadamichi Kuribayashi, had ordered them to build a series of tunnels,

**Boats carrying Marines and supplies sped toward the beaches of Iwo Jima during the opening hours of the battle.**

concrete bunkers, and caves. When the Marines began landing, most of the Japanese were well hidden in these defensive positions. Under their commander's orders, they didn't attack immediately. They waited for more waves of Marines to come ashore.

Marines unloaded supplies after landing on the beaches of Iwo Jima.

So as the Marines landed, the island was quiet. One of them later recalled what he was thinking. "I was confident," he said. "I thought this was going to be a cinch." But soon the Japanese opened fire on the Americans, cutting them down by the dozens. Many of the defenders were on Mount Suribachi. This volcano, at the southern tip of the island, was the highest spot on Iwo Jima. Japanese artillery and machine guns hidden on Suribachi fired down on the beach below. As more Americans landed, they saw the bloodied bodies of the dead and wounded blocking their path.

## Planting a Flag

Suribachi quickly became a key target for the Marines. Fighting on and around the volcano went on for several days. Finally, on the morning of February 23, a platoon of 40 Marines began a slow climb up Suribachi. The mountain was not tall—just 550 feet (168 meters) high. But it was steep, and only one path provided an easy route to the top. The platoon advanced slowly, not sure whether it would face

Marines tried to take out enemy positions as they made their way up Mount Suribachi.

a sudden explosion of Japanese bullets. The shots, though, never came. When the men reached the top of the volcano, they searched for something to use as a flagpole. They had carried a U.S. flag with them up Suribachi. They tied it to a tall metal pipe the Japanese had left behind and set the pipe in the ground. For the first time in World War II, the Stars and Stripes flew over land that Japan had controlled before the war.

The raising of one country's flag over another's land is a sign of victory. For the Japanese, seeing the U.S. flag over Iwo Jima was another sign that they had little chance to defeat the Americans. And for the Marines and sailors on and around the island, the flag meant hope. Remembering the sight of the flag, Marine Max Haefele said, "It felt great. … There was a lot of noise all over the island." The news of the flag raising had spread quickly, sparking cheers from the American forces.

The flag raising, though, also stirred some of the Japanese still hidden on top of Mount Suribachi. A few fired shots from their hiding places, and both sides tossed grenades. After several moments, the fighting ended. The Marines used their grenades and flamethrowers to take out the remaining Japanese soldiers.

Suribachi seemed to be secure for the Americans, but two Marine officers weren't happy. They wanted another flag on top of the mountain—a bigger one. Soon a second team of Marines reached the top of the mountain. The flag they carried was 4 feet 8 inches (1.4 m) tall and 8 feet (2.4 m)

"It felt great. ... There was a lot of noise all over the island."

wide. It was big enough, as one Marine at the top later said, so everyone "on this whole cruddy island can see it." With the aid of a Navy corpsman, the Marines tied the new flag to a pole. As they put it up, several other men took down the first flag. Six men, working together, raised the new flag, and an Associated Press photographer, Joe Rosenthal, caught the moment on film. His photo of the second flag raising on Iwo Jima soon became one of the most famous images of World War II. The photo captured just a small event, but its importance to the country was immeasurable.

**Joe Rosenthal's photograph of the second flag raising on Iwo Jima became an icon of bravery and hope during wartime.**

# ANOTHER FAMOUS BATTLE FLAG

*Francis Scott Key saw the U.S. flag flying over Fort McHenry from the deck of a ship in Baltimore Harbor.*

Cameras did not exist in 1814, when British ships threatened to destroy Baltimore, Maryland. Francis Scott Key had to use words to capture the moment when U.S. defenders in Fort McHenry drove off the British during the War of 1812. Key, a lawyer, was on a ship in the harbor when the British attacked the fort. During the nightlong battle, the Americans flew a small flag over the fort. On the morning of September 14, with the fighting over, Key stepped onto the ship's deck and saw that the flag was still there. The fort commander then raised a much larger flag, 42 feet (13 m) by 30 feet (9 m). He wanted all of Baltimore to know that the city was saved.

Key wrote a poem about the battle and the U.S. victory. Key wrote that, even as bombs burst and rockets flew, the U.S. flag had remained over the fort. His poem was set to a well-known tune, and the new song was called "The Star-Spangled Banner." Today Americans know it as the National Anthem. The image Key created with words still stirs pride in the U.S. flag and the men and women who defend it on the battlefield.

## ChapterTwo
# CONQUEST AND REVENGE

The historic moment photographed on Iwo Jima came near the end of World War II. But for several years before it, American soldiers, Marines, sailors, and airmen had been fighting the Japanese in the Pacific Ocean. In 1931 Japan had invaded and taken control of part of China. U.S. political leaders opposed the Japanese action, but they were not ready to go to war so far from home. Through the 1930s Japan made plans to take over more of China, then seize lands in Asia that were controlled by European nations. The Japanese wanted natural resources, such as oil and rubber. Conquest seemed the easiest way to get them.

Most Americans in the 1930s were more concerned with problems at home than with events in distant Asian lands. In October 1929 the country entered the Great Depression, the worst economic period in U.S. history. Millions of people lost their jobs and their homes. And after seeing the horrors of foreign war during World War I (1914–1918), many U.S. lawmakers were desperate to avoid any more wars, unless the United States was directly attacked.

## Pearl Harbor and Beyond

By the end of the 1930s, Asia was not the only continent threatened with war. In Europe, German leader Adolf Hitler and his Nazi Party had built a massive and powerful military force. Hitler thought Germany had given up too much land

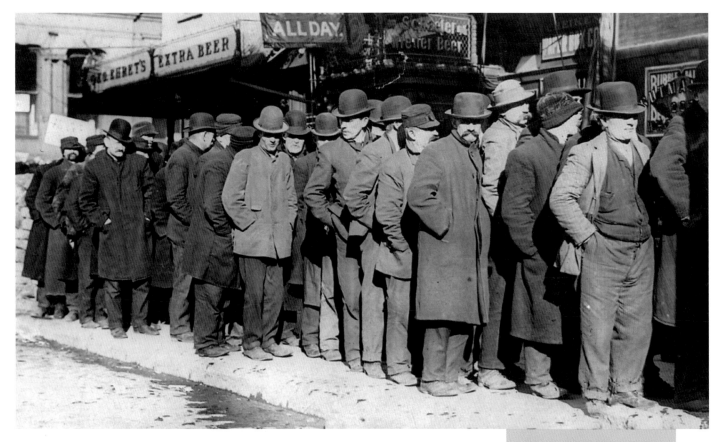

**Men waited in line for a 5-cent meal during the Great Depression.**

after losing World War I. He wanted to take it back—
and more.

Germany's invasion of Poland on September 1, 1939,
marked the start of World War II. U.S. President Franklin
Roosevelt saw the threat that the Germans and Japanese
posed to freedom and safety around the world. He wanted
to help the nations fighting them. But most Americans still
wanted to stay out of foreign wars. The Japanese finally
ended that reluctance.

The Japanese feared a U.S. attack on their military, since
they knew the Americans would eventually challenge their
control of much of Southeast Asia and China. To strike the

first blow, Japan sent hundreds of warplanes to attack U.S. ships docked at Pearl Harbor, Hawaii, on December 7, 1941. It was a Sunday morning, and many people were getting ready for church when they first heard the enemy planes. People scrambled outside, and the island's defenders tried to shoot down the low-flying bombers. The Japanese force, however, was too large and too quick. The attack killed or wounded more than 3,000 Americans, destroyed 149 planes, and left 20 warships damaged or destroyed. The next day Roosevelt asked Congress to declare war on Japan. Soon the United States was also at war with Germany and its ally, Italy.

**The Japanese attack on Pearl Harbor prompted the United States to enter World War II.**

Many in the United States already had a negative view of the Japanese. Racist feelings had led the country to limit immigration from Japan. And Americans had heard stories of the violent deaths of civilians in China. To some, the Japanese seemed less honorable than Americans, and not to be trusted. But even with these views, Americans were stunned by the surprise attack on Pearl Harbor. The negative opinions now exploded—along with a strong desire for revenge. A college professor said he hoped citizens would get angry: "We need to arouse a permanent and effective anger in our people … one which can be kept alive for the purpose of doing our job, which is beat the other fellow." President Roosevelt assured the country, "No matter how long it may take us … the American people … will win through to absolute victory." He said the United States had a "righteous" cause—it had a right to punish the Japanese for their hateful act of war.

As Japan attacked Pearl Harbor, it also began assaults on several European colonies in Asia. The Japanese also attacked the Philippines, which was then under U.S. control. By the spring of 1942, Japan seemed to have a commanding position in the Pacific. The lands it controlled on the mainland of Asia provided natural resources. Small islands in the ocean provided ports for its ships and airfields for its planes. To defeat Japan, the United States and its allies needed to push the Japanese out of the lands they had conquered. Then the Allies could mass forces in those lands to prepare for an attack on Japan itself.

"No matter how long it may take us … the American people … will win through to absolute victory."

## The Call to War

The Japanese attack, along with German victories in Europe, stirred Americans to take action. The war affected everyone, whether they served in the military or not. As millions of men and some women joined the military, other Americans stayed behind to build the weapons and prepare the supplies that U.S. forces would need. To make sure the factories had enough raw materials, people had to limit or end their use of some goods, such as rubber, nylon, and gasoline. Families raised vegetables, and children helped collect scrap metal that could be used to build planes or tanks.

**At school young people were taught about the importance of collecting scrap materials for the war effort.**

Early in 1942 President Roosevelt addressed the nation. He spoke just after George Washington's birthday, reminding the country of the bravery and determination of Washington and his army as they won American independence. Now, facing threats from Germany and Japan, Roosevelt called for all Americans to unite in an even harder battle.

Roosevelt said the war was meant to punish nations that attacked others for no reason. The war was also a battle to protect freedom. Americans wanted to defeat the Japanese and Germans to stop them from causing further harm around the world. Victory would make the United States and the world more secure. But for many Americans, defeating the Japanese was also about revenge for the attack on Pearl Harbor.

The U.S. Navy won its first major victory over the Japanese in June 1942. U.S. fighter planes destroyed several large Japanese warships off the island of Midway. Admiral Chester Nimitz said the victory was partial revenge

"Vengeance will not be complete until Japanese sea power is reduced to impotence."

## ROOSEVELT'S CALL FOR UNITY

On February 23, 1942, President Roosevelt told the nation's radio listeners:

"[George] Washington's conduct in those hard times has provided the model for all Americans ever since. ... He held to his course, as it had been charted in the Declaration of Independence. He and the brave men who served with him knew that no man's life or fortune was secure without freedom and free institutions. The present great struggle has taught us increasingly that freedom of person and security of property anywhere in the world depend upon the security of the rights and obligations of liberty and justice everywhere in the world. ... We Americans will contribute unified production and unified acceptance of sacrifice and of effort. That means a national unity that can know no limitations of race or creed or selfish politics. ... Never before have we been called upon for such [an extraordinary] effort."

**Navy fighter planes left many Japanese ships burning off Midway Island.**

for Pearl Harbor. But he said that "vengeance will not be complete until Japanese sea power is reduced to impotence." By beating Japan, the United States would restore the sense of pride and confidence that had been destroyed at Pearl Harbor. Americans would show the world that they could defend themselves and defeat any enemy.

## War in the Pacific

Hearing the words of Roosevelt and other leaders, Americans understood the importance of the war. They knew everyone had to work together. Newspapers, movies, radio shows, cartoons, and posters stressed the need for everyone to do their part. But the Marines, soldiers, and sailors in the Pacific would have the bloody task of actually defeating the Japanese. U.S. military leaders drew up a plan that relied heavily on the Marines. They would sail to islands held by the enemy, launch amphibious assaults, and try to gain control of the land.

**Marines were briefed on the plan to take Iwo Jima from the Japanese.**

The first invasion came in August 1942, in the Solomon Islands. The fiercest fighting took place on Guadalcanal, where the Japanese were building an airfield. If they succeeded, Japanese planes could attack Allied ships carrying troops, weapons, war supplies, and other goods. The fighting on and around Guadalcanal went on for six months before the Marines and Navy finally forced the Japanese to flee. As the fighting went on elsewhere, the courage of the Marines became obvious. They had to fight an enemy that had greater resources, and troops who would rather die than surrender. Over the next three years, Americans saw the Marines' bravery again and again.

## On to Iwo Jima

By 1945 the Marines had taken a series of Pacific Islands that the Japanese had occupied during the war. Each victory brought the Americans closer to their goal: building airfields that could send bombers to attack Japan. The first air attacks had begun in 1944 from bases in China, but the Japanese were closing in on them. With the Japanese navy weakened, it would be much easier for Americans to defend the island bases. Flights from those bases finally began in November, as B-29 bombers took off from the Marianas Islands.

That airfield was not perfect. The route from there to Japan was long, and the large bombers had to carry plenty of fuel. That meant they could carry fewer bombs. The distance also made it hard for a damaged plane to safely return to the Marianas for repairs. The military needed a base closer to the Japanese mainland. The new base would provide an emergency landing place for damaged bombers. It would also support the fighter planes that flew along with the bombers to protect them from enemy fighters.

Iwo Jima already had an airfield, which the Japanese could use to attack the bomber bases in the Marianas. If the Americans controlled the island, they and not the Japanese would have that important field. The island is just 750 miles (1,207 kilometers) from Tokyo and about halfway between Japan and the Marianas. Admiral Nimitz made his decision: He wanted Iwo Jima.

The Japanese saw the value of the tiny island as well. By June 1944 they realized the Americans would come for Iwo Jima. One night General Kuribayashi walked to the beach near Mount Suribachi. Iwo Jima is shaped like a large pork chop, and the volcano is at the tip of the chop's bone. Kuribayashi looked out at the sea and said, "The enemy must land here. He has no alternative." The spot would provide the least difficult amphibious landing area, where the Marines could quickly set up a base. They would first want to take Suribachi and the high ground near it, to keep the Japanese from firing down on them.

Kuribayashi prepared to defend that spot and the rest of the island. In the months that followed, his men built underground tunnels that linked bunkers. They built rooms where soldiers slept and officers planned for war. All the time, the Americans were flying more and more planes to attack Iwo Jima, to prepare for the land assault. The bombs

**Located at the southern tip of the island, the volcano Suribachi is the highest point on Iwo Jima.**

**"The enemy must land here. He has no alternative."**

sent clouds of sand and volcanic ash skyward, but they did not touch Kuribayashi's underground defenses.

If the Americans were fighting for revenge, the Japanese had their own reason to show tremendous courage. Their country had a tradition of brave warriors. The Japanese thought it was nobler to die fighting or commit suicide than to surrender to an enemy. The men on Iwo Jima had a special duty, Kuribayashi said. "We are now in the front line of the national defense," he said. "We must do everything we can for the Emperor, for the personnel already perished in the war, and for the people of the homeland." The Marines would face an enemy that would do anything to stop them.

## The Battle Begins

Many of the Marines had already fought the Japanese during other amphibious assaults. Others had only trained in Hawaii and had not seen battle. All knew the difficulty they faced on Iwo Jima. February 19, 1945, was their D-Day—the day to go ashore. That first day, the fighting went on for hours, with planes overhead, U.S. ships targeting Japanese defenses, and both sides on the island firing their guns, large and small. Mount Suribachi quickly became a key target for the Marines. About 2,000 Japanese were scattered across

Marines landed on Iwo Jima while cruisers, destroyers, and other U.S. ships waited at sea.

the volcano, firing down on the Marines. As the day went on, more Marines came ashore, and they worked to surround Suribachi. Taking the mountain would be tough. The Japanese were ready to die in their caves and bunkers after killing as many Marines as they could. The Marines would have to advance on the hiding places one by one, risking many lives in the process.

By the third day of the invasion, the Marines were just 200 yards (183 m) from the main Japanese defenses on Suribachi. The Americans prepared for a major assault, knowing that the unseen Japanese were waiting with guns of all kinds. One Marine later said, "There seemed nothing ahead but death. If we managed to survive the first part of the attack, we would only become targets for Suribachi's concealed guns."

Moving forward, the Marines heard the Japanese bullets and artillery shells flying all around them. They saw friends drop to the ground, wounded, dying, or already dead. But the Marines didn't stop. Some fired their guns at the small holes the Japanese peered through inside their concrete bunkers. When the Japanese moved away from the holes, other Marines ran up to drop in a grenade. Then a whoosh of fire from a flamethrower made sure all the enemies inside were dead.

This slow, deadly combat went on through the day. On all sides of the volcano, the Americans crawled along, knocking out the Japanese defenses. At times, though, the Japanese simply left one bunker and used tunnels to hide in another.

"There seemed nothing ahead but death."

A bunker the Marines thought they had silenced by killing the enemy inside would suddenly come back to life. That night the Japanese were still on the mountain, and still dangerous. General Kuribayashi sent out soldiers he called prowling wolves. Their mission: Sneak up on the Americans during the darkness and kill them silently with bayonets. The "wolves" struck several times that night.

Wounded Marines were treated at first-aid stations on Iwo Jima.

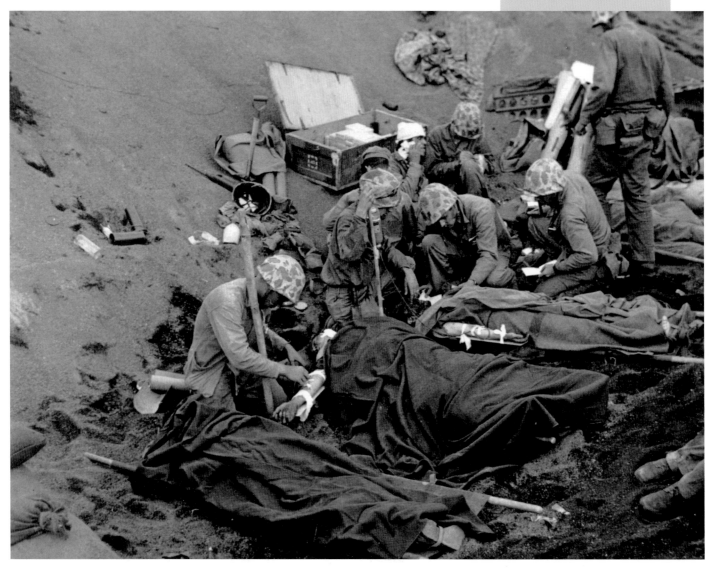

The next morning the Americans prepared to move farther up Suribachi. Most of the Japanese defenders remained in their caves and bunkers. One group, though, fled their defenses, hoping to join another Japanese force away from the volcano. Once they were in the open, the Americans easily cut down most of them. An American commander had already decided that the Japanese were too weak to hold on to

**Marines displayed Japanese flags outside an enemy cave they captured.**

Suribachi. The next day the Marines would climb to the top of the volcano.

When they reached the top, two groups of Marines planted U.S. flags. The picture of the second one became famous. It did not just capture a moment of victory against a strong foe. It also represented the effort every Marine had made since the first assault on Guadalcanal in 1942. The rising flag over what had been Japanese land meant that the Americans who had died had served a higher purpose. They had made their country proud again. To some Americans, the image might have also suggested the bravery of all U.S. soldiers through the years, back to the men who fought for George Washington during the American Revolution.

The image of the flag raising at Iwo Jima was quickly sent around the world. The description sent with the photo was simple, explaining the "who, what, where, and when." But Americans saw the symbols and ideas the picture held. They did not need anyone to explain the deeper meaning.

## REPORTS ON THE BATTLE

On February 25, 1945, *The New York Times* reported on the fighting at Iwo Jima:

"By noon our forces were reported to be gaining ground slowly. ... In every zone of the fighting the enemy resisted our advance to the full extent of his armament. Weapons of the 'bazooka' type were employed against our tanks and the use of rocket bombs weighing about 500 kilograms [1,100 pounds] continued. ... In the south Marines continued their mopping-up of enemy strong points in and around Mount Suribachi. Incomplete reports indicate that 115 enemy [positions] have been destroyed in that sector. A total of 2,799 enemy dead have been counted on Iwo island."

# FINISHING THE BATTLE

*In March 1945 U.S. ships and planes still plied the waters and air around Iwo Jima, trying to rout the Japanese.*

Today the flag raising and the famous photo of it are what most people remember about the Battle of Iwo Jima. But the struggle to take the island went on for another few weeks, because the Japanese had solid defenses across the island. Some of the strongest bunkers could only be destroyed by the large naval guns offshore, but the Americans didn't want to risk killing their own men by using such weapons. The firing and the bombing from planes had to be precise. On the ground some of the worst fighting came on the northeast part of the island. The Americans called one particularly well-defended area the "Meat Grinder," since they suffered so many losses there.

By the end of March, the Americans finally had complete control of Iwo Jima. More than 6,000 Americans had died, and almost 20,000 were wounded. All but about 1,000 of the 21,000 Japanese defenders had died in combat or committed suicide. Iwo Jima was the first battle during World War II in which the Americans had more casualties than the Japanese.

## ChapterThree
# FIGHTERS, FLAG, AND PHOTO

Six men strain and lean and move forward. Two are hidden from the viewer's eyes, but the men are there, working together for a common goal: to raise their country's flag for everyone on Iwo Jima to see. The six men didn't know that their simple act would become such a historic moment. Soldiers had raised other flags on other islands before. Americans had done it earlier in World War II. But this flag raising was captured on film. And the men's bodies and the flag came together in a special way—a way that made Americans proud of their armed forces, their flag, and their country.

## Who Raised the Flag?

When the Iwo Jima picture first appeared in newspapers, the U.S. government didn't know which six Americans raised the flag. Their names, and how they got to that spot on Mount Suribachi, were reported later. The flag itself had come from a landing craft, then had been passed through several hands until it reached Private First Class Rene Gagnon. He was a runner, someone who carried messages if a two-way radio was not available. Officers had wanted Gagnon to carry batteries to a radio operator on top of the volcano. At the last minute, someone handed Gagnon the flag too. As the world later learned, the flag had once flown on a ship that docked in Pearl Harbor, Hawaii. A sailor had found

The famous flag was damaged by the strong winds atop Mount Suribachi. Today it is on display at the National Museum of the Marine Corps, south of Washington, D.C.

it in a storage room there, the place where the war had begun for the United States.

On his way up the mountain, Gagnon joined a four-man patrol led by Sergeant Mike Strank. He and his men were going to lay down a telephone wire that would run from the top of the mountain to a camp below. With Strank were Corporal Harlon Block and Privates First Class Ira Hayes and Franklin Sousley. The five Marines reached the top and told others about the order Gagnon had been given to put up a new flag.

Already at the top was Navy Corpsman John "Doc" Bradley. He and other corpsmen went into battle with the Marines to treat the wounded. Sergeant Strank asked Bradley to help with the flag raising. The flag was tied to a heavy pipe that the Japanese had used to drain water.

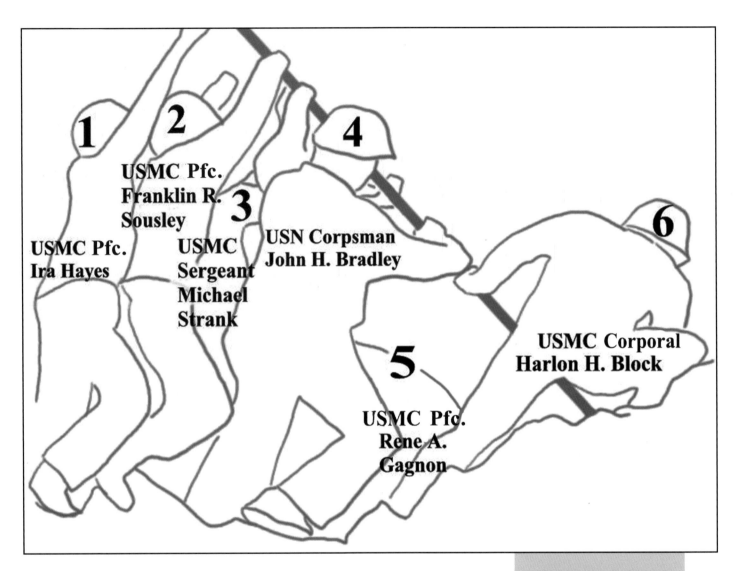

1 — USMC Pfc. Ira Hayes

2 — USMC Pfc. Franklin R. Sousley

3 — USMC Sergeant Michael Strank

— USN Corpsman John H. Bradley

4

5 — USMC Pfc. Rene A. Gagnon

6 — USMC Corporal Harlon H. Block

With the flag attached to the pole, the six men struggled to put it up. The wind blew hard that day on top of Suribachi, and the ground was covered with stones. They shifted easily under the flag raisers' feet. But after a few seconds, the pole was secure and the flag was up. The Marines on and around the volcano barely noticed the second flag raising. One later said, "We didn't think it was a big deal at all." But Joe Rosenthal thought the flag raising would make a good picture. His photo of the event is the one the world knows today.

The men captured in the famous photo were soon identified and hailed as war heroes.

Joe Rosenthal's photo of the second flag raising on Iwo Jima has been called "the most beautiful picture of the war."

## The Right Place, the Right Time

Joe Rosenthal had been a newspaper photographer in San Francisco, California, when Japan attacked Pearl Harbor. He tried to volunteer for the military, but weak vision kept him out. Instead Rosenthal joined the U.S. Maritime Service, which trained sailors for merchant and Army transport ships. By 1944 he was working for the Associated Press, which provides news and photos for hundreds of U.S. newspapers. For the AP, Rosenthal had taken photos at several Pacific battles against the Japanese before coming to Iwo Jima.

Though he was never an official Marine photographer, Joe Rosenthal was made an honorary Marine in 1996.

World War II was closely reported by U.S. newspapers and radio networks. Americans were eager for news about the fighting overseas. The U.S. government allowed reporters and photographers to travel with the troops. But the government also screened the information before it was released. Military officials did not want the enemy to learn anything about U.S. plans for the war, or the losses they suffered. At times weeks passed before the reporters could give all the news. Sometimes the journalists censored themselves and reported nothing. They did not want to report negative news that might hurt American morale.

The military also had its own reporters and photographers. Some of their reporting was used in newspapers and magazines published just for the troops. The government also wanted a complete record of what happened during the war. Film crews traveling with the troops recorded battles, and clips from these films were shown in movie theaters around the world. The government coverage of the war was a form of propaganda—information meant to persuade people to hold certain beliefs or to take certain actions. During World War II, much of the propaganda was meant to keep Americans working hard to support the war. The government also tried to describe events in a way that made the country look good and the enemy look weak or evil.

As an AP photographer, Joe Rosenthal tried to capture the truth of the war, as he saw it. Of course, he could only be in one place at a time, so he could only shoot a small part

of the action. And he didn't always see the most dangerous parts of a battle, since, as he later said, "you are only ... in the way." But several times he faced difficult conditions where he could have been killed by enemy fire. And on Iwo Jima, he saw the mangled bodies of dead Marines soon after the first assault. With the Japanese still hidden all around the island, Rosenthal's job was not an easy one.

## Taking the Picture

On the morning of February 23, 1945, Rosenthal went to photograph a top U.S. government official who had come to Iwo Jima. Rosenthal later met with two Marine photographers. He told them about a planned flag raising at the top of the volcano. Rosenthal persuaded the two armed Marines to go with him up Suribachi. On the way, another Marine photographer, Louis Lowery, told them they were too late. The flag had gone up, and he had taken pictures of it. But, Lowery said, the view from the top was good, and so the other three men continued their climb.

Reaching the top, Rosenthal felt a bit of pride as he watched the flag blowing in the breeze. Then he noticed Sergeant Strank and several other Marines preparing to put up the second flag. As they strained to put up their pole, others stood ready to take down the first flagpole. Rosenthal tried to position himself so he could get all of the new pole in his frame. He held the camera so it would take a horizontal view of the scene. Corporal Harlon Block crouched low on the ground, where the pole would stand. Strank held the flag around the pole so it would not flutter and get in the men's way. Privates First Class Rene Gagnon and Franklin Sousley and Navy Corpsman John Bradley each took a spot along the pole, and Pfc. Ira Hayes stood at the rear. Without even looking through his camera's viewfinder, Rosenthal pressed the shutter. In just a few seconds, the second pole was up. Rosenthal's camera caught just a tiny fraction of the brief event.

Rosenthal took a few more pictures that day. Then he shipped his film to the island of Guam to be developed. Unlike photographers today, using digital cameras, Rosenthal had no way of knowing what image he had captured during the flag raising. On February 25 the flag-raising photo began to appear in newspapers across the United States. The reaction to Rosenthal's work was immediate—and powerful. One writer compared it to the paintings of the great Italian artist Leonardo da Vinci. Another called it "the most beautiful picture of the war."

# THE OTHER PHOTOGRAPHER

*Louis Lowery's photo of the first flag raising on Iwo Jima is not as well known as Rosenthal's photo.*

Louis Lowery never won the fame Joe Rosenthal did. Lowery had been on top of Suribachi for the first flag raising. He took a picture of Marines surrounding the flag after putting it up. Lowery was low on the ground, so the flag towers over him. Above his camera and below the flagpole, a Marine crouches with his rifle. The wind whips the flag straight out, making it easy to see all of its stars and stripes. The image shows a sense of victory, with the clear view of the flag. Yet the armed Marine suggests the volcano is a dangerous place, as he scans for possible enemy troops. Soon after taking the photo, Lowery fell and broke his camera. He still managed to save the film.

Rosenthal's photo of the second flag raising created a greater sense of energy and emotion, leading to its fame. Afterward, Lowery admitted that Rosenthal had taken the better picture. But he was angry that he was ignored as the photographer who took the pictures of the first flag raising on Iwo Jima.

Within a few days, Rosenthal heard that one of his pictures was becoming famous, but he didn't know which one. He had taken a later picture of a group of Marines around the second pole. He assumed that one was the picture appearing in all the papers. He didn't find out until he reached Guam in early March. The flag-raising picture had been cropped so that now it was vertical. The focus was on the flag and the men beneath it. Rosenthal had placed his camera so only the sky was behind the men and the flag. The light background gave the objects in front greater depth and force. Seeing the final version, Rosenthal did not think his work was so extraordinary. But the image had a huge impact, as he soon learned. And over time he saw the importance it held. The photo did more than record a brief moment. It gave Americans renewed pride.

## The Meaning of the Picture

In 2000 James Bradley's book *Flags of Our Fathers* was published. He is the son of John Bradley, one of the flag raisers. The book later became the source for a successful movie of the same name. In his book, Bradley describes how Americans felt when they saw Rosenthal's picture: "The flag raising photograph signaled victory and hope, a counterpoint to the photos of sinking ships at Pearl Harbor that had signaled defeat and fear four years earlier."

Over time Rosenthal began to understand the many messages his photo contained. Any photo has one literal meaning—it shows the appearance of objects or people

"The flag raising photograph signaled victory and hope ..."

# THE PHOTOGRAPHER SPEAKS

*Joe Rosenthal posed with his famous photo in 1985, 40 years after the event.*

In 1992 Joe Rosenthal spoke to the authors of *Shadow of Suribachi*, a book describing the events on Mount Suribachi:

"I positioned myself to get a flag going up. ... To raise myself a little bit, I found some old sandbags and a couple of rocks, and I pushed them together. ... I got up, and I figured that would be about it. [Marine cameraman William] Genaust came across in front of me, ... saying as he did, 'I'm not in your way, Joe?' I turned and said, 'No, Bill.' By being polite to each other we almost ... missed it. 'There it goes, Bill!' I caught it out of the corner of my eye. ... I swung my camera up. Steady. Just time enough. Got to get it. It's on its way. Then it all came together. The wind caught the flag and passed it over the figures. Perfect!"

that are in front of the camera at a certain moment. But some photos have deeper meanings. Rosenthal, studying his work, saw that the men seemed to be in action as they strained to raise the pole. A still image, like this one, can suggest great movement and effort. And that effort is focused on a common goal—presenting a symbol of America for all to see. Rosenthal also noticed the ground by the men's feet: "The disrupted terrain and the broken stalks of the shrubbery exemplified the turbulence of war." But despite the turbulence, the flag raisers achieved their goal.

Over time people found other meanings in the photo. The various family backgrounds of the raisers reflected some of the diversity found in America. Rene Gagnon was a New Englander who traced his roots to French-speaking Canada. Harlon Block came from a small Texas town, and Franklin Sousley was another southerner, from the hills of Kentucky. Ira Hayes was a Native American, of

The flag raisers (left to right): Rene Gagnon, Harlon Block, Franklin Sousley,

the Pima tribe. Michael Strank had settled in the United States after leaving his native Czechoslovakia. John Bradley was from rural Wisconsin. Some of the men were Roman Catholic, while others were Protestant. Americans liked to say their country was a melting pot, creating one united society out of people from many backgrounds. The six men who raised the flag on Mount Suribachi seemed to represent that idea.

Even at this early point in the battle for Iwo Jima, the U.S. casualties were high. Because of that, Rosenthal's image was not just about the living fighters' winning a victory. It also honored those who died at Iwo Jima and throughout the long war. The photo came at an important time for the civilians back home. The United States and the Allies seemed to be winning in both Europe and the Pacific. But the war had dragged on for more than three years. The civilians had suffered too, as they worked many

**Ira Hayes, Michael Strank, John Bradley.**

# OUT OF THE MELTING POT

*African-Americans fought in World War II but were segregated from white troops.*

The famous flag-raising photo doesn't show a member of an important group of Americans—African-Americans. At the time the U.S. military was segregated—black people and white people lived separately and did not fight side by side. About 900 black Marines took part in the assault of Iwo Jima. They were not front-line troops, but many played key roles driving the amphibious trucks that brought supplies ashore and bringing ammunition to the front lines. The 2006 movie *Flags of Our Fathers*, about the Iwo Jima flag raising, upset some African-Americans. They realize no black people helped raise the flag, but the movie mostly ignored the role they played during the battle.

## "A picture like that is a real gift."

hours, worried about their friends and loved ones, and went without favorite foods and goods. The families of the dead had lost relatives they would never see again. The triumphant photo of the flag offered them hope during a bleak time. Marianne Fulton, an expert on photography, described the impact: "You're worried about your life, your family, the future of the nation, and this really incredible picture of strength and determination comes out. A picture like that is a real gift."

The flag itself, not just its raising, also stirred people who saw the photo. The Stars and Stripes has been a symbol of the United States since the American Revolution. The Pledge of Allegiance, recited in schools, shows the role it plays in creating the sense of being American. During World War II, Americans flew flags from homes and other buildings as never before. The flag was a reminder of what the country was trying to do: defend freedom and destroy evil. The Rosenthal photo reinforced the idea that the flag shaped the identity of Americans, people from different backgrounds but with common goals.

As time went on, Rosenthal understood the importance of his image. But he didn't think it was important that he took it. Anyone could have taken the photo, he later said, "but the Marines took Iwo Jima." They were the real story. But the picture quickly took on a life of its own.

# ChapterFour
# THE LASTING EFFECT

Across the United States, Americans immediately
responded to the photo from Iwo Jima. Newspapers that ran
Rosenthal's image received thousands of calls from people
who wanted more copies of the photo. Some papers released
special versions of it on cardboard, so readers could frame it
and hang it in their homes. Never before in history had one
photo produced such a strong, positive reaction.

U.S. government officials realized that the flag-raising
photo produced a sense of patriotism. They also saw the
melting pot of servicemen who were represented in it. They
stood for Americans from all parts of the country. They
were average Americans working together. The government
quickly began to use the image in various ways. It appeared
on a postage stamp and was turned into a poster that
encouraged people to buy war bonds. The government used
the money from the sale of bonds to pay for the war effort. In
the future the bonds' buyers would get their money back plus
a little more. President Roosevelt wanted to go beyond the
image. He ordered the men in the photo to come back to the
United States and help sell the bonds.

Only three of the flag raisers were able to help with
the sale. Strank and Sousley were dead, and Block was
still not known to be one of the raisers. But he too had
died in combat. Hayes, Gagnon, and Bradley were the
three who would help sell the bonds, becoming famous in

A 3-cent stamp was issued in 1945 to commemorate the raising of the U.S. flag on Iwo Jima.

the process. They toured the nation, meeting movie stars and political leaders, including the new president, Harry Truman. (Roosevelt had died a few months earlier.) The men reminded Americans that the war in the Pacific was far from over. Buying bonds was important to help the country win.

## From Photo to Sculpture

Describing his famous photo, Joe Rosenthal said the position of the men almost made them look like a sculpture. Throughout history, some artists have tried to capture an instant of motion in marble or bronze. A sculpture lets viewers walk around the art and experience it from every side. They can touch it, and perhaps better imagine themselves as part of the scene.

# UNWELCOME FAME

As the years passed, John Bradley stopped talking about his experience as one of the Iwo Jima flag raisers. He gave his only interview for a 1985 film about the event. He said, in part:

"If I knew what was going to come of that photo, I am sure I would not have jumped in and given them a hand putting that flag up. ... I could do without the pressure and the contact by the media. I'm just a private man and I'd like to leave it that way. ... We certainly were not heroes."

Others who saw Rosenthal's image also noticed its sculptural feel. One of them was Felix de Weldon. An immigrant from Austria, de Weldon was in the Navy when the photo appeared. Trained as an artist, he began to work with clay to try to duplicate the photo as sculpture. In June 1945 he showed a small model of his work to President Truman. De Weldon hoped the government would help him build a larger one for the public to see.

By November de Weldon had completed a version of his statue that was larger than life. Made of clay and plaster, it was placed outside in Washington, D.C. Because of the plaster that covered it, the statue would not survive long in the rain, wind, and snow. But de Weldon already had plans for a bronze statue that could survive any weather. And the new one would be even bigger. With help from the Marines, the artist began his project.

De Weldon had the surviving flag raisers sit as models. He used photos of the other three to help him make the work as accurate as possible. Money for the statue came from current and former Marines, companies, and private citizens.

Felix de Weldon (left) posed with the surviving flag raisers—Gagnon, Hayes, and Bradley—next to the clay and plaster version of his statue.

Finally, in November 1954, de Weldon's work was dedicated at Arlington National Cemetery, just outside Washington, D.C. The image from Mount Suribachi became the center of a memorial honoring all Marines killed in battle. From its base to the tip of the flagpole, the statue stands almost 80 feet (24 m) tall. Each of the Marines is 32 feet (9.7 m) tall. A real U.S. flag flies from the pole.

**The larger-than-life memorial sculpture honors the bravery and sacrifice of fallen Marines.**

By the time the statue was done, the United States had gone through another war. The Soviet Union and China had backed North Korea's invasion of South Korea, a U.S. ally. Americans feared other wars would erupt, fueled by the Soviet Union's desire to spread its influence and power. Vice President Richard Nixon spoke at the dedication of the Iwo Jima statue. He said the image from Suribachi "symbolizes the hopes and dreams of America and the real purpose of our foreign policy. ... There is no greater challenge to statesmanship than to find a way that such sacrifices as this statue represents are not necessary in the future."

## Raising the Flag Again and Again

De Weldon's statue was not the only one based on the Iwo Jima photo. Other sculptors created their own. The image was even re-created using flowers and placed on floats that appeared in the famous Rose Bowl Parade. At some public events, veterans or other patriotic citizens dressed in military uniforms and posed as the six flag raisers.

The event on Mount Suribachi inspired entertainers as well. Soon after the photo appeared in 1945, a song came out called "Stars and Stripes on Iwo Jima." Some of the lyrics said:

> When the Yanks raised the Stars and Stripes
> on Iwo Jima Isle,
> Ev'ry heart could sing once again
> And the sight of Old Glory over Iwo Jima Isle
> Swelled the hearts of our fighting men.

Motion pictures also showed the fighting on Iwo Jima and the flag raising there. The 1949 movie *Sands of Iwo Jima* starred the actor John Wayne and featured Hayes, Gagnon, and Bradley in several scenes. The flag that the three helped raise was also used in the movie. *Sands of Iwo Jima* was popular with moviegoers and won an Academy Award, the highest honor for a movie.

Decades after the Battle of Iwo Jima, another film appeared. The 2006 movie *Flags of Our Fathers* focused on the six flag raisers and how the photo changed the lives of the three survivors. Hayes, Bradley, and Gagnon were called heroes, but they knew the true heroes had died on Iwo Jima. Hayes, in particular, struggled with his fame. He died 10 years after the war, at age 32. His story was later turned into *The Outsider,* a 1961 movie. His story

*Sands of Iwo Jima* tells the story of a group of Marines from training through the Battle of Iwo Jima, during which they witness the famous flag raising.

was also told in song. Johnny Cash took "The Ballad of Ira Hayes" to number 3 on *Billboard*'s country music chart. But most Americans wanted to remember the pride stirred by the original photo, not any problems that arose after it.

## Was the Photo Faked?

One of the biggest problems involved the photo itself—how and why it was taken. Almost as soon as it first appeared in public, some people wondered whether Joe Rosenthal had faked or staged the photo. A reporter for *Time* and *Life* magazines said the picture was staged after the first, "real" flag went up. When Rosenthal first discussed his picture, he did not mention the first flag raising, because he thought most people knew about it. He was not trying to pretend it hadn't happened. He added to the confusion when he said that a picture he took of the flag and some Marines on Suribachi was staged. He had asked some Marines to stand around the raised flag and cheer, to show they were happy with their victory. He was referring to this later photo, not his famous one, when he said the photo was staged.

After people accused Rosenthal of staging the picture, he tried to explain what had happened. He said the flag raising was not the first. And he added, "I did not select this spot for the second flag. I did not select the men for the picture. I did not in any way signal for it to happen, but I was aware that it was going to happen."

Slowly the facts came out. Rosenthal had photographed Marines carrying out an order to take down the first flag and

"I did not in any way signal for it to happen, but I was aware that it was going to happen."

Four of the six flag raisers—Bradley, Hayes, Sousley, and Strank— also appear in Rosenthal's later, posed photograph.

put up the bigger one. Nothing was staged for the purpose of creating a photograph. Defending Rosenthal, another photographer said it would have made sense to have the raisers look at the camera, if it had been staged. Newspaper editors liked to identify local boys fighting overseas. But none of the men's faces are visible, which added to the photo's impact. They could be any six Americans, and thus they could stand for all Americans.

Rosenthal said it wouldn't have been "a disgrace" if he had staged the photo, rather than record reality. But he didn't. He admitted he was lucky, with "the wind rippling the flag right, the men in fine positions, and the day clear enough to bring everything together into sharp focus." For his luck, Rosenthal won the Pulitzer Prize, the highest award for American journalists.

But in the decades that followed, Rosenthal had to keep denying the charge that his photo was not real. The Marines had added to the questions by not saying much about the first flag raising and the photos of it. Maybe Marine officials did not want anyone to think Rosenthal's image was not a true record of events. Perhaps they feared people would think Rosenthal was simply seeking to become famous by creating such a powerful shot. Or perhaps they feared people would think the government had tried to stir emotions and create propaganda. Part of the photo's power came from knowing Rosenthal had snapped the image as it happened, and had captured something that said so much about the United States. Any suggestion the photo was fake would weaken that power.

As late as the 1990s, the notion that Rosenthal's picture was staged still sometimes appeared in the media. The truth, though, quickly overcomes those false ideas.

## An Enduring Image

Today the Iwo Jima image can easily be found in books and on the Internet. Visitors to Arlington National Cemetery can walk around the statue it inspired. The image of the flag raising is so well known that artists have used it in various settings. It appears often in political cartoons, which newspapers publish to comment on current events. In some cases people who are not Marines hold the flagpole. In others the flag isn't even present. Just the position of the six flag raisers suggests the famous photo. The cartoonists refer to the historic image because of its place in history. They know readers will automatically think about the pride and patriotism it stirs. In some cases, cartoonists are suggesting that the government is betraying values Americans hold dear. In other cartoons the artists want viewers to think about the bravery of the Marines on Iwo Jima. The cartoonists are suggesting that the event they are showing is worthy of the same respect.

Companies have used the image in advertising. Advertisers hope the emotions the picture stirs will be linked with their products or services, so people will be more likely to buy them. Some people, though, don't like ads that use the image. They want to remember the Iwo Jima photo as a historic, proud moment. They don't want it associated with a product. In 2009 a Spanish oil company released an ad showing the Marines raising a checkered flag. Such a flag is waved to show the winner of a car race. Some Americans criticized the ad.

The photo of the Iwo Jima flag raising has been called an icon—an image that becomes a lasting symbol of something important. Because of its emotional power, the photo will continue to inspire other uses. Of all the pictures taken during World War II, the flag raising on Iwo Jima remains the most famous. Americans still cherish what it represents: bravery, sacrifice, success, unity, and pride.

Joe Rosenthal's photograph of the second flag raising on Iwo Jima may be the most reproduced photograph of all time.

# Timeline

Japan invades and takes control of part of China; the United States opposes the action but is not ready to go to war.

**1931**

**September 1–3, 1939**

Germany invades Poland, beginning World War II.

**December 7, 1941**

Japan launches a sneak attack on the U.S. Navy base at Pearl Harbor, Hawaii; the United States enters World War II.

Rosenthal's picture appears in newspapers across the country and wins instant fame.

**February 25, 1945**

**March 1945**

Three of the flag raisers are killed in combat.

### February 19, 1945

U.S. Marines begin an amphibious assault on the Japanese island of Iwo Jima.

### February 23, 1945

AP photographer Joe Rosenthal photographs the second raising of a U.S. flag on Mount Suribachi, Iwo Jima.

The three surviving flag raisers return to the United States as heroes to help sell war bonds; Rosenthal's picture appears on posters to help sell bonds.

### April 1945

### June 1945

Felix de Weldon shows a model sculpture of the flag raising based on Rosenthal's photograph.

# Timeline

## 1949

The movie *Sands of Iwo Jima* portrays the battle there and the historic flag raising.

## 1954

The U.S. government dedicates the U.S. Marine Corps War Memorial, which features a larger-than-life-size sculpture of the flag raising.

## March 1995

U.S. and Japanese veterans hold a memorial service on Iwo Jima on the 50th anniversary of the invasion.

## April 13, 1996

Joe Rosenthal is made an honorary Marine.

## 1961

The life of flag-raiser Ira Hayes, who died in 1955, is depicted in the movie *The Outsider*.

Johnny Cash's version of the song "The Ballad of Ira Hayes" reaches number 3 on *Billboard*'s country music chart.

## 1964

## 2000

*Flags of Our Fathers*, a book about the Iwo Jima flag raising written by the son of one of the flag raisers, is published.

## 2006

The movie version of *Flags of Our Fathers* is released in theaters; Rosenthal dies at 94.

# Glossary

**ally**: friend and supporter, especially during wartime; when *Allies* is capitalized, it refers to the United States and its allies during a war

**amphibious**: describing a land invasion using soldiers transported on ships and boats

**artillery**: large, mobile guns

**bayonet**: blade attached to the end of a rifle and used as a weapon in close combat

**bunkers**: protected rooms or spaces, usually underground and often made of concrete

**casualties**: soldiers killed, captured, missing, or injured during a war

**censored**: restricted the printing or broadcasting of certain information

**defensive**: protective against an enemy attack

**flamethrower**: weapon that projects a burning stream of liquid

**grenade**: handheld explosive weapon thrown at an enemy

**impotence**: lacking in power, strength, or vigor

**propaganda**: information spread to try to influence the thinking of people; often not completely true or fair

**statesmanship**: attempt between nations to settle their problems without using force

**turbulence**: great commotion or agitation

# Additional Resources

## Further Reading

*American Flag Questions and Answers.* New York: Smithsonian, 2008.

Beller, Susan Provost. *Battling in the Pacific: Soldiering in World War II.* Minneapolis: Twenty-First Century Books, 2008.

Bradley, James, with Ron Powers. Adapted for young people by Michael French. *Flags of Our Fathers: Heroes of Iwo Jima.* New York: Laurel-Leaf Books, 2006.

Nelson, S.D. *Quiet Hero: The Ira Hayes Story.* New York: Lee & Low Books, 2006.

Dougherty, Terri. *Raising the Flag: The Battle of Iwo Jima.* Mankato, Minn.: Capstone Press, 2009.

## Internet Sites

Use FactHound to find Internet sites related to this book. All of the sites on FactHound have been researched by our staff.

Here's all you do:
Visit *www.facthound.com*
Type in this code: 9780756543952

# Source Notes

Page 6, line 2: James Bradley with Ron Powers. *Flags of Our Fathers.* New York: Bantam, 2000, p. 154.

Page 8, line 14: Ibid., p. 205.

Page 9, line 2: Parker Bishop Albee Jr. and Keller Cushing Freeman. *Shadow of Suribachi: Raising the Flag on Iwo Jima.* Westport, Conn.: Praeger Publishers, 1995, p. 51.

Page 14, line 10: "After the Day of Infamy: 'Man-on-the Street' Interviews Following the Attack on Pearl Harbor." December 1941. Library of Congress. 12 July 2010. www.loc.gov/teachers/ classroommaterials/connections/pearl-harbor/ history3.html

Page 14, lines 13 and 16: "A Date Which Will Live in Infamy." North Carolina Digital History. 12 July 2010. www.learnnc.org/lp/editions/nchist-worldwar/5844

Page 16, sidebar, line 3: Franklin D. Roosevelt. *Selected Speeches, Messages, Press Conferences and Letters.* New York: Holt, Rinehart and Winston, 1964, pp. 307–308.

Page 17, line 1: Richard Wheeler. *Iwo.* Edison, N.J.: Castle Books, 1980, p. 15.

Page 20, line 17: Ibid., p. 33.

Page 21, line 8: Ibid., p. 135.

Page 23, line 12: Ibid.

Page 26, sidebar, line 3: "The Text of the Day's Communiqués on Fighting in Various Zones." *The New York Times.* 25 Feb. 1945, p. 2.

Page 30, line 7: *Shadow of Suribachi,* p. 51.

Page 34, line 2: Ibid., p. 55.

Page 36, line 10: *Flags of Our Fathers,* p. 211.

Page 38, line 20: Ibid., p. 220.

Page 39, sidebar, line 4: Richard Goldstein. "Joe Rosenthal, Photographer at Iwo Jima, Dies." *The New York Times.* 21 Aug. 2006. 12 July 2010. www.nytimes.com/2006/08/ 22/obituaries/22rosenthal.html

Page 40, line 8: *Shadow of Suribachi,* pp. 60–61.

Page 43, line 6: Mitchell Landsberg. "Fifty Years Later, Iwo Jima Photographer Fights His Own Battle." February 1995. Associated Press. 12 July 2010. www.ap.org/pages/about/pulitzer/ rosenthal.html

Page 43, line 24: "Joe Rosenthal, Photographer at Iwo Jima, Dies."

Page 46, sidebar, line 5: *Flags of Our Fathers,* p. 257.

Page 49, line 7: Karal Ann Marling and John Wetenhall. *Iwo Jima: Monuments, Memories, and the American Hero.* Cambridge, Mass.: Harvard University Press, 1991, pp. 17 and 19.

Page 49, line 22: "Star and Stripes on Iwo Jima." Bob Wills.com. 12 July 2010. www.bobwills.com/ lyrics/stars_stripes.html

Page 51, line 21: *Shadow of Suribachi,* p. 75.

Page 52, line 9: *Iwo Jima: Monuments, Memories, and the American Hero,* p. 80.

Page 53, line 1: Ibid.

# Select Bibliography

Albee, Parker Bishop, Jr., and Keller Cushing Freeman. *Shadow of Suribachi: Raising the Flag on Iwo Jima*. Westport, Conn.: Praeger Publishers, 1995.

Altman, Alex. "Were African Americans at Iwo Jima?" *Time*. 9 June 2008. 12 July 2010. www.time.com/time/nation/article/0,8599,1812972,00.html.

Bradley, James, with Ron Powers. *Flags of Our Fathers*. New York: Bantam, 2000.

Brinkley, Douglas, ed. *World War II: The Allied Counteroffensive, 1942–1945*. New York: Times Books, 2003.

Edwards, Janis L., and Carol K. Winkler. "Representative Form and Visual Ideograph: The Iwo Jima Image in Editorial Cartoons." *Quarterly Journal of Speech*, vol. 83 (1997), pp. 289–310. 12 July 2010. www.comm.umd.edu/faculty/tpg/documents/EdwardsWinkleronIwoJima.pdf

Goldstein, Richard. "Joe Rosenthal, Photographer at Iwo Jima, Dies." *The New York Times*. 21 Aug. 2006. 12 July 2010. www.nytimes.com/2006/08/22/obituaries/22rosenthal.html

Haskew, Michael E., ed. *The World War II Desk Reference*. New York: HarperResource, 2004.

Landsberg, Mitchell. "Fifty Years Later, Iwo Jima Photographer Fights His Own Battle." February 1995. Associated Press. 12 July 2010. www.ap.org/pages/about/pulitzer/rosenthal.html

Leary, Kevin. "Joe Rosenthal: 1911–2006." Sfgate.com. 21 Aug. 2006. 12 July 2010. http://articles.sfgate.com/2006-08-21/news/17307868_1_flag-raising-picture-iwo-jima-joe-rosenthal

Marling, Karal Ann, and John Wetenhall. *Iwo Jima: Monuments, Memories, and the American Hero*. Cambridge, Mass.: Harvard University Press, 1991.

Poor, Jeff. "Iwo Jima Veterans Blast Time's 'Special Environmental Issue' Cover." Business and Media Institute. 18 April 2008. 12 July 2010. www.businessandmedia.org/articles/2008/20080417171532.aspx

Roosevelt, Franklin D. *Selected Speeches, Messages, Press Conferences and Letters*. New York: Holt, Rinehart and Winston, 1964.

"The Text of the Day's Communiqués on Fighting in Various Zones." *The New York Times*. 25 Feb. 1945, p. 2.

Trachtenberg, Alan. *Reading American Photographs: Images as History, Matthew Brady to Walker Evans*. New York: Hill and Wang, 1989.

Wheeler, Richard. *Iwo*. Edison, N.J.: Castle Books, 1980.

Willmott, H.P., Robin Cross, and Charles Messenger. *World War II*. New York: DK Publishing, 2004.

# Index